In the Days of Our Seclusion

March – May 2020

NATHAN BROWN

MEZCALITA
PRESS

FIRST EDITION, 2020
Copyright © 2020 by Nathan Brown
All Rights Reserved
ISBN-13: 978-1-7348692-1-7

Library of Congress Control Number:
2020942680

No part of this book may be performed,
recorded, thieved, or otherwise transmitted
without the written consent of the author and
the permission of the publisher. However,
portions of poems may be cited for book
reviews—favorable or otherwise—without
obtaining consent.

Cover Design: Jen Rickard Blair

Mezcalita Press, LLC
Norman, Oklahoma

In the Days of Our Seclusion

March — May 2020

NATHAN BROWN

Table of Contents

March ... .
A Calculated Distance ... 5
The Side-effects ... 7
How Serious ... 10
To the Hoarders ... 11
What She Didn't Mean ... 13
The Chalice and the Snail ... 15
Gone Viral ... 17
Wondering While I Wander ... 19
The Father, the Son, and the Holy ... 21
Making Poets ... 23
A Little Room ... 24
Why the Osage ... 26
The Phoenix ... 28
Here, in the Chaos ... 31
What Now? ... 34

April ... ...
A Dog-Eat-Deer World ... 39
Fragile ... 42
Someday You Will ... 44
Someday We Will ... 46
Transitioning ... 48
Out of the Blue ... 51
Pills & Spells ... 53
Categories . . 55
Deep Thought, and Other Supercomputers ... 57
Social Distancing ... 59
Slouching Towards Heaven ... 61

She Calls It Prayer ... 63
What Not ... 65
Shelter-in-Place ... 66
What I Should Really Tell My Therapist Is: ... 69
On the Rebound ... 85
Again, for the First Time ... 87
Back to What? ... 89
One, at Least ... 92
Honor Thy Mother ... 94
Too Quiet ... 96
Wireless ... 98
Phantom Opera ... 99
The Last Haboob ... 101
Earth Day ... 105
A Strange Gap ... 107
Stepping Out ... 108
Just a Visitor Here ... 110
Involunteer ... 113
Cliffhanger ... 115
More than Your Parents Want Me to Say ... 119
Quarantoonie ... 122
If You Care ... 124
Well, Hello ... 126
Yes, Hello ... 128
Lucky? ... 130

May ... ...
Bother ... 135
Thousand-yard Stare ... 137
You Talkin' to Me? ... 139

Unspoken ... 141
AK-47s into Plowshares ... 143
And 40 Nights ... 145
Where Do We Begin? ... 146
Quietly, Softly ... 148
Here's to You ... 150
All Lakes Great and Small ... 152
What the Hand Knows ... 155
What Luck ... 156
And Why Not? ... 158
Praise Be .. 160
Foresight ... 162
Hope ... 164
Silent Mode ... 167
All the Wheres out There ... 169
The Days Are Too Much with Us ... 171
Better than No Place ... 172
A Hint of Vermouth ... 175
Where the Magic Is ... 177
Hope Springs ... 179
The Newness ... 181
What Makes Sons ... 183
Like It Is .. 185
The Effect It Has ... 188
Dancing with Saint Vitus ... 190
Oh, Jonathan ... 192
The Ritual ... 193

Introduction

Around the Ides of March—the day before my 55th birthday—I was beginning to sense that Rome would never be the same. The news turned ominous shades of fire, while emails and texts began to let me know I would not be traveling as much this year as I am used to. One by one, the lights went out in the city of my career, and income. Every reading, conference, workshop, and music gig I had scheduled from April forward began to drop off the calendar, and I felt a strange mix of both thrill and fear at the prospect of being homebound for a time. But when I wrote the check for my half of the next house payment, I knew what hell awaited me come June… or maybe July. Even poets can do the math when there is only "outgo."

One evening, in those early days, Ashley was having a Zoom Happy Hour with two longtime friends in Houston and Denver, Sarah Flournoy and Liz McIlravy. I mention their names because the concept for this project—of writing commissioned poems for a donation of some kind—was their idea. And what I owe them, I haven't quite calculated yet. But that "idea" has turned out to be the saving grace of my 2020, and career.

No exaggeration. I couldn't have imagined the effect and reach this would eventually have.

So it is that I've now completed the first book in what will be a series. *In the Days of Our Seclusion* contains the poems that came out of March through the end of May—the first "season" of this new time, a new era, we are now living in, and through. They reveal our awakening to the great change in reality that looks to be our foreseeable future. Many of these pieces have blinking eyes and big question marks on their faces. And they will, I hope, serve as solid reminders of this critical period as we move forward into what looks to be an age in which we will have to reinvent culture.

An unexpected, but delightful, side-effect of the project has been The Fire Pit Sessions, a series of live online readings of the poems that have served well to feed the fire of requests and commissions. So far, these are available on Facebook Live, and every one of them can be viewed on my personal page:

https://www.facebook.com/chinacoman

Acknowledgements

This book is dedicated to my wife Ashley, and her friends, Sarah Flournoy and Liz McIlravy, who were its cocktail-infused instigators.

That said, I also have to dedicate it to all the good souls who commissioned poems and donated to the cause. Without a doubt, those donations have preserved our home and life here in the Texas Hill Country. We would not be making it without them. And our gratitude to all of you is deep, very deep, and ongoing.

A special thanks, though, to Ashley, for putting up with the intrusion and time commitment of The Fire Pit Sessions we film maybe a bit too regularly.

And thanks, as always, to my parents, Lavonn and Norma Brown, for your never-ending support. And also to my daughter, Sierra, you've been in this game, and putting up with me, your entire life. Sorry Hon'...

And to Jen Blair? Your artwork plays a huge role in so many of my publishing endeavors. Many thanks to you for that.

Also, thanks to *Wimberley Living Magazine* for first publishing the poems "Wondering While I Wander," "What the Hand Knows," and "Unspoken."

Lastly, I would like to offer a special thank you to Cristina McQuistion. You have been an exceptional supporter of the Pandemic Project, and I am very grateful.

In the Days of Our Seclusion

MEZCALITA
PRESS

March ... ...

To register what it feels like to be
alive in a particular moment in
history is an enormous task.

> ~ Stephen Dunn
> *Degrees of Fidelity*

A CALCULATED DISTANCE

> Wednesday, March 18

To suddenly be forced
to do a thing I'm fond of,
reminds me of a confusion
I spent most of my teens
brooding down inside.

I loved a good book,
but… I did not want
some English teacher
telling me which one
I had to read… and,
especially by what date
I had to have it finished.

I continued to feel the same
all the way through the great
confusion of getting a Ph.D.

And so it is that being told—
by some hijacked radio station,
or jumpy television screens—
I must now keep a calculated
distance from other citizens,
and that complete isolation
would be an even safer bet,

stirs up the dormant coals
of those pubescent fires
of rebellion I used to
burn all over town...

even though I'm being
told to do the very thing
I had set as a goal in life.

The Side-effects

> Thursday, March 19

They say you can see
farther through the smog
over in Shanghai these days.

And, that dolphins have been
spotted frolicking in the slightly
bluer canals of Venice once more.

The stock market's getting a chance
to see what trading would be like
if all of us woke up to the idea
that we do not need most
of the nothing we own.

Academic conferences
have all been canceled,
as well as departmental
and committee meetings.

The great mass of a man
in a stained John Deere
hat and muddy overalls
who made fun of a lady
ahead of us for hoarding,

as we all suffered through
the grocery line, actually
caught the stench of his
irony, when he plopped
his 24-pack of cheap beer
down on the conveyor belt.

Making love doesn't have to be
as carefully planned or scheduled
around the job and running errands.

I have a lot more time to contemplate
that one particular comma in that
one particular poem. Put it in.
Take it out. Think about it.

Our President has more
opportunities to award
himself a '10 out of 10'
for how well he is doing
in handling the pandemic.

Congress may be forced
to act upon some thing.

Evil officials, bad actors,
double agents, dictators,

foreign, and domestic,
have eased up efforts
to destroy the world,

permitting a dangerous
opportunity to confront
their eroded consciences.

I, on the other hand, have
more time to spend alone
with my thoughts—one
potential catastrophe.

And worse, for you,
there's nothing to stop
a poet from sitting here
and writing second poem.

How Serious

> Saturday, March 21

Even the sun has gone
behind the frightful curtain
of this mandatory quarantine.

Three days, nothing but clouds
parsing out long gray sentences
of rain on our gray metal roof.

And I think the sun realizes,
if it doesn't pull through,
then none of us will.

To the Hoarders

> ~ for Sam Lanham
> Monday, March 23

So, my father grew up
using the Sears catalogue,
if you know what I mean…

and those of you who grew up
in houses with bathrooms, may
not. But he knows what I mean.

His mom grew the green beans,
the beets, and the cucumbers
they ate or pickled for later.

And she picked the plums,
the peaches, the blackberries
they preserved in Mason jars.

Eggs didn't come by the dozen
in Styrofoam boxes, they came
straight from the chicken's ass.

Grandma made soap out o' lye
and lard from the big fat hog
they slaughtered in the yard.

Which should tell you where
they got the bacon and ham
from, if you catch my drift.

So… the 500 rolls of toilet
paper stuffed in the closet,
and all the eggs n' produce

stashed in your fridge, will
only prolong your demise…
when the real trouble comes.

What She Didn't Mean

~ for Chuck Smith
Tuesday, March 24

"Love is like a virus…"

O Maya, dear Ms. Angelou,
never has your famous quote
sounded so… unsettling…

"Love is like a virus…"

and, in a crazy number
of ways, I have to add.
Because, depending on
which strain, that sucker
can take you down, hard.

"Love is like a virus…"

and, I have this friend
who came down with
a pretty bad case of it.
The unrequited kind.
The coronal variation
that burns in a halo—

a rarefied and gaseous
envelope, that engulfs
the heart and the head.

"Love is like a virus…"

and, unless we control
the spread of the pain
it leaves when it goes,
closing the borders,
maintaining a sane
distance… it can,
so quickly, turn into
a pandemic of the soul.

"Love is like a virus…"

but, those who survive
the shakes and fever
are stronger for it.

The Chalice and the Snail

~ for Chuck Baker
Tuesday, March 24

The snail carries his palace
on his back, an unpretentious,
mobile kingdom he lords over.

And in the faith of snails, it also
serves as a holy chalice, the only
sacred cup he would ever need.

While all around him, the birds
flutter and fluff their plumage,
the bees get drunk on mead,

lizards flash their stripes
and speed, and butterflies
flex that yellow and orange.

But what does he wont for
all that color and currency,
their pomp and pretention?

He carries what his shoulders
can bear… and he carries it
at his own ordained pace.

Some might call him lesser.
And yet... there he sits...
carved into eternity...

there on the outer shell
of the Chalice of Antioch,
in the Metropolitan Museum

of Art, alongside Christ,
a lamb, and an eagle,
wings spread wide.

Gone Viral

> ~ for Cristina McQuistion,
> and the Oklahoma Symposium's 20th Year
> Wednesday, March 25

We're gathered there together,
in all of those previous years
out in the Oklahoma hills,

with enough memories
to carry us through
this wild cancellation.

We did enough thinking
then, to sustain the losses
of a Twentieth Anniversary.

But let us not forget, friends,
what it means to be the only
hope of a great, but battered

state—the state of my raising,
the state of my heart, the state
where they'll spread my ashes

when this, or the next, thing
comes to take me down…
if you'll have me back.

But, this year, when
the bells of April toll,
I am afraid we will all

have to drink too much
in the shelter of our own
places, the familial spaces

we've chosen to ride it out.
I'm raising a toast right now
to the north in the dusky sky:

> *May we all hold on tightly*
> *to the things we must not lose,*
> *and may all of us've smartly*
> *stocked up on our booze.*

Wondering While I Wander

> ~ for Elizabeth Dennis (and kids)
> Thursday, March 26

When I was young...

   (that actually happened
      long, long ago... but,
      ssshh... don't tell...)

a favorite way to wander,
so I could wonder
about things,
was to walk
in the woods.

My gosh, for hours
I would walk and wonder
as I wandered in the woods.

But, on days when I couldn't
wander in the woods, because
you can't wander in the woods
every single day... can you?

   (I mean, seriously, how
      crazy would that be?)

Anyway, what I'm saying is,
I had to learn how to wander
in the wilderness of my mind.

And, let me tell you… it is
wild in there… there in
the woodsy wilderness
of my Willy-Wonka head.

> (I mean, let me tell you,
> there's more than just
> a chocolate factory
> at work in there.)

And, that wild-and-wonky
wilderness is the reason I have
111 journals on the shelves near
my Willy-Wonka head, all filled
with the Crayon-magic-marker-
glue-stick wonderings that came
from the wanderings in my mind.

The Father, the Son, and the Holy

> ~ for George McQuistion, on turning 60
> Friday, March 27

As you wheel your way
into this brand new decade,
I plod half way through mine.

At 55… I trust your last five years
have been more organized, efficient,
and useful to society than my next

five are likely to have been
when I turn the same
landmark corner.

I can only hope
mine does not arrive
on the heels of a pandemic.

And because of that, I'm afraid
you will not get to retire, this year,
from being a great husband and father.

We have to pull together in times like
these. So, I'll bet you 60 bucks
they ask you to stay on…

they'll need their MacGyver
more than ever, as well as all
the music and bad dad jokes.

Don't ever stop with the jokes,
and the music. For all our sakes.
When the songs and the laughter

fade, the whole shebang is done for.
They speak more to the four noble
truths than we silly poets ever do.

So congratulations on living longer
than most poets tend to, as well.
Something you probably knew,

being that Renaissance Man
you are. And... any advice
you could offer for my next

five years, how to be a better
father for my daughter, and son
to my parents, would be appreciated.

Making Poets

~ for Lander Bethel
Friday, March 27

This season will go deeper
than just a cut. This one's
gonna slice some meat off.

It's when hunkering down
for our darkest hour is not
the metaphor it used to be.

It's just the black, billowing
cloud of the truth we have yet
to face in shrouded days to come.

The balance in my checking account is
$300-something—the lowest I have
allowed it to get in over 30 years.

I'm used to digging in my pockets
for spare change, but the real truth,
the harder one below money-level…

is the soul-check that's coming soon…
one that inches the blade closer to bone.
The truth that asks how committed we are.

A Little Room

~ for Candace Mary Osterhout
Saturday, March 28

There is a wicked-strange
silence to city streets
not being used.

I can't imagine
the Bronx right now,
a stillness it's never known.

And yet, not all isolations
are the same. I just heard
a cow moo, by the creek.

And though an occasional
car passes in the distance,
someone off to a nowhere

I often imagine people here
in the Hill Country are off to,
it's mostly doves and cardinals.

This time of the year is always ripe
with the chatter and oak-tree clatter
of baby-making among the feathery.

Looking for a mate never goes out
of style. And I appreciate the one
I found. But, we also never plan

on never not being around them.
We try to create space as we shelter-
in-place, and to create within that space.

But any amount of space, in any place,
can get tight when we cannot leave it.
Love has its limits, after all… No?

So, I've taken to walking alone,
or with the cows, by the creek,
and then writing on the porch.

I have no idea what my friend
in the Bronx is doing about it.
But… my wife seems grateful.

Why the Osage

> ~ for Don Verser, from Sarah Flournoy
> on their 4th Anniversary
> Sunday, March 29

Sunday mornings
come in quietly here
in our neck o' the hills.
So, during a quarantine,
the stillness of it verges
on something Paleolithic.

I can hear the inchworm
grunting as he climbs his
invisible rope up to the tip
of a long leaned-over blade.

This is a perfect time to love
the one you love, along with
the birds and the trees, the
plants and the bees, more
than most other people.
It's a short trip for me.

So if you like the one
you're locked up with
as much as I like mine,
we're both lucky bastards.

Add to them, long walks out
in the woods, on the prairies,
hikes that end in the shaking
of cocktails or pouring wine,
and... well... I would raise
a toast to every last bit of it.

So, here's to one who knows
why the Osage Hills are sacred,
 why it's hard for me to leave
Black Mesa, and its horny
little toads, once I've taken
the trouble to drive that far,
 why I cannot shake that red
dirt from the entangled roots
of that tiny little town where
my father chased a milk cow
alongside a chat road at dusk,
 why Donald Trump is such
a menace to all these things,
 and why I'll have to chain
myself to a prickly pear
cactus in the grasslands
of northern Oklahoma,
when he comes for it all.

The Phoenix

~ for Linda Barrett
Monday, March 30

In a season of ashes,
when the great bird
has landed in its fire
once again, we survey
the smoking remains...

the number of the dead,
dying, and those waiting,
increasing in thick tendrils
up to a dark and roiling sky,

China still lying about their
toll-rate... New York City
making no mistake about
the nightmares still ahead,

states closing their borders
with each other... almost
forgetting about Mexico,

high-risk parents hunkered
in the den of the two-story
I grew up in on the plains,

where they can barely climb
their own set of stairs, stare…
wondering if the carton of milk
or the potatoes they just bought
curbside will be the carrier, and
deliverer, of their final notice,

my strict instructions to "not"
drive up to be with them there,
both the fridges and the freezers
are full… if it happens… then,
it happens… they will "not"
request medical attention,
and the three of us boys
can come up together
to retrieve their ashes
when this thing's over.

And now I begin to worry
that things I've worried over
for the last thirty years've been
a waste of my time. And I spent
some of my best years, dammit,
worrying about all those things.

But, soon enough, I will begin
to let that go. I will pull myself

together. Then, I will remember
some old prayers I used to know.

And, the prayers will remind me
that ashes are the way of Earth.

But also, that the same is true
of rebirth. And, that is when
I will go to sit among those
ashes, pass the peace pipe,
and wait for the return
of that great bird.

Here, in the Chaos

~ for Linnea Cavitt
Monday, March 30

Before the noun 'chaos'
meant "A gaping void,
yawning gulf, a chasm,
abyss," or also "…utter
confusion and disorder"
in the Oxford English
Dictionary,
        the Greeks
considered him the first
of the primordial deities
that preceded the creation
of the universe. Married to
Nyx, the Night, who gave life
to Gaia, Tartarus, Eros, and
Erebus—Earth, Hell, Love,
and Darkness.
        My God.
Those Greeks never fail
to be more dramatic
and beautiful than
the dictionary.

And their version
rings a helluvalot truer

to the chaos we now find
ourselves sailing around in...

the coronavirus, with its crashing
waves, storming seas, and Sirens
singing their beguiling songs
so filled with sexy lies...

sailors dashing ships
against razor rocks
just to put an end
to the torture...

sufferers who
can never return
to the same country
and home they had left.

Yes, Gaia has had enough
of all this human nonsense...
and she's gonna give us a good
body check. A little something
hard to remind us that we are
not all that necessary to her
much grander schemes...
she has ample options.

Hell awaits the Great
Pumpkin, and all of his
Father-fearing followers
who would not recognize
the Antichrist, not if it bit
their asses in the Garden.

Love will, surely, hold out
for any and all who remain
with their compassion intact,
after every heart's been tested.

And Darkness… as Darkness
is prone to do… will, when
it understands it's time,

recede.

What Now?

> ~ for Terri Stubblefield
> Tuesday, March 31

What does a plague matter
to my friend who recently
lost her friend and lover
for the last forty years?
A friend who also lost
a daughter to a crime
they've never solved.
You think a pandemic
scares her, after all she's
had to stand or stare down?

So, now a virus insists that she
distance herself from those few
people who remain for comfort.
Tell me… which prayer of hers
should God respond to first?

And the poet in me knows
to quit with that question.
The friend in me, though,
needs to go ahead and say:

I don't know if God's heard
your petitions yet… as he is

receiving an unprecedented
number of calls these days.

But, my dear friend Terri,
my prayer for you, if I still
have an idea what a prayer
might be, is that your feet
find the bottom to rest on.

That you make it through
the days of creeping death
and this ordered seclusion.

That you may see your way
with the one dim headlight
you have left… to someday
break out into some healing,
and more beautiful, other side.

April ... ...

Change is a stubborn backseat driver.

~ Loretta Diane Walker
Ode to My Mother's Voice

A Dog-Eat-Deer World

~ for Barbara Blanks
Wednesday, April 1

A viral thing has descended,
swooped down and in on us,
like some apocalyptic cliché
of a colossal storm cloud
in one of Hollywood's
box-office lacklusters.

Now we are choking
on its invisible poison.
We're all bunkered down,
like the Gestapo is outside,
which... it may... soon be?

So, we're left with nothing
but time to be smothered
by the news, and ongoing
body count. the cinematic
images of New York City
we can't believe are not
starring Kurt Russell
wearing that eyepatch.

Each morning we awake
to the same frightened cat

wrapped around our face
that's begging to be fed.

And, in the bare pantry
we discover we are out
of her favorite food, so,
we've got to suit up to go
to the grocery store where
a growing number of fellow
suffocators sport the latest
in medical protective gear.

Which brings me to a walk
in the woods this afternoon.
I came upon a deer chewing,
which is all deer're ever doing,
unless they're pooping, and so,
I was glad this one was chewing.

He did not care, not in the least,
about my rather close proximity.
And, if deer are able to smirk…
that's exactly what this one did.

He smirked at me. As if to say,
with his face, "Havin' fun friend,
back there in humanland?"—as if

to say, "Yeah... we did it, buddy.
We concocted this just for you."

As if to say, "And I speak for
all the animals of the planet.
And I think that you know
what I mean." And, it was.
Mean, I'm meaning to say.

But, I know what he means.
And yet I'm not one to stand
around in the woods and argue
with a snarky deer. So I smirked
right back, and I think he caught
the drift on my face, the hint...

that if things get bad enough,
this nonpracticing vegetarian
might just make an exception.

Fragile

> ~ for Debora Chappell
> Wednesday, April 1

> On and on, the rain will say,
> how fragile we are.
> ~ Sting

There is a teepee I made
 of long cedar posts back
  in the half-acre wood
   on our extra lot...

 I like to write there
  in the veil of a thing
  held together only by
the delicacy of gravity.

Coming into it just now
 I walked right through
  a spider's web that I
   didn't see in time.

  It had no chance
  against my size and
  brief panic...   a whole
night's work lost in a flash.

You don't have to tell my dad
at 86, taking nearly 20 pills
each 24 hours, just how
quickly we can go…

that's why each time
he goes to get up out of
his recliner… he pauses…
to think it through for a second.

That's why I feel genuine guilt
over the tiny lone star tick
I just turned to blood
on this white page.

The same sad reason
I almost tripped earlier,
trying not to step on a line
of honest, hardworking ants.

Someday You Will

> ~ for Lou Kohlman
> Thursday, April 2

> Though the world is torn and shaken
> Even if your heart is breakin'
> It's waiting for you to awaken
> And someday you will –
> Learn to be still
>
> ~ Don Henley & Stan Lynch

The clouds have dropped in,
come down to join us in shelter,
so low, they throw the sounds of
a trash truck some ten blocks over
and a chainsaw across the valley
right up onto my front porch.

They could rain any minute now,
as if a conductor's baton is raised,
a stillness verging on the bizarre…
wrens, head-cocked and peering up,
parched oaks with their leaves peeled,
thirsty roots hushed with anticipation.

For a long time, I've claimed to be
in search of more silence in life.

After many failings, I converted
to the softer idea of seeking quiet.

I now believe my desires might be
wrapped up in the one for stillness.

We have a wider array of ways to die
than ever before in our human history,
as well as a much larger variety of sweet
distractions along the path to that grave.

But our atoms… bless their little nuclei…
weren't designed to stress without ceasing.

They are begging to take a coffee break,
"Please, dear God, sit your asses down,
turn off that infernal news… the birds
have been singing for 60 million years,
trees whispering for 300 million more,
and they are dying… for an audience."

Someday We Will

> ~ for Loretta Diane Walker
> Thursday, April 2

For those sheltered-in-love,
remember that Odessa…
whether the Ukraine
or West Texas…
can be one Hell
of a desolate forty
days n' dark nights
in the heart's desert—
especially for a soul alone
walking circles 'round a small
kitchen table, or tiny cul-de-sac,
circling into a near nonexistence.

There's no alone like the alone of
healing from the spiritual scars
of cancer, while still reeling
from the cancerous scars
left on the spirit—burned
in by the searing emptiness
of that acid mind gone dead
to the waves of its own rage.

So remember, the next time
your someone touches you,

all of the possible ways we
can touch and be touched.

Remember that, for some
in this airborne isolation,
they need every type that
we can find in the toolbox.

This's going to be a lengthy
and a very treacherous road
back to any last remnant of
anything resembling home.

So, let's make sure to reach
down for every hand we see
reaching up. Be sure we are all
in the wagon when we get there.

Transitioning

> ~ for Julane Borth
> Friday, April 3

A rift in the species?
              Maybe.
A bone-level change?
                It comes.
Will it come easy?
              Never does.

As a baby from the mid-60s,
I've not experienced change
like what lies ahead now...

a sea change in the genome
sequence of a generation
and all those yet to be.

I harbor an ounce or two
of hope that humans might
actually become more human,
though I fear the opposite looms,
like Grendel struggling to cover
his ears in the back of his cave.

We are not good at this game.
One of total transformation.

Like velociraptors protesting
the coming of that meteor.

Back in '83, I graduated
high school with a guy
who only recently—or,
maybe I mean, finally—
discovered—or, maybe I
mean came to grips with—
the sense that he is a woman.

And, maybe I had my own sense
of that in him for the 30-plus years
it took for the ordained transition.

I felt what I'd call a quiet relief.
Others demonstrably did not.
I mean, Norman, Oklahoma,
well, it ain't no South Beach.

But he is out on the radiant
other side of things now…
a beautiful new being…

and I heard heaven sigh,
as I believe it always does,
when the world is translated

into a better place by someone
creating a better space to live in.

And I saw a fatherly God smile,
as I believe God always does,
at the revival of a small town
that thought it couldn't do it.

And then I think to myself,
as I always eventually do,

Yes...   that...

    that right there,
        could save
the human race.

OUT OF THE BLUE

~ for Jessica Wells Packard, and Jayden
Friday, April 3

Some skip up to us…
spring into our lives…
like spirits.. or sprites
sprung from a mystical
forest, little beings that
we know are more than
mere children… spunky,
devious angels sneaking
away from heaven, just
to mess with our heads
the best way they can.

They roll by on skates
or bicycles… throwing
kisses and punch-kicks
with the same zany love
they hold for life itself.

Black shades and spiky
blue hair… you'd best
watch your back, Bud.

They have middle names
like Harley, and've never

met a stranger. They give
a dog a bone and a name
like Alabaster so they can
nickname it Allie Bastard.

They are here. They are
that wild child we both
love and fear. And so,

we hold on, tight,
for dear life.

Pills & Spells

~ for Tammy Franklin
Saturday, April 4

Doctors can't afford
to ever let us know
just how much they
simply do not know.

So they lie like parents
who do it for the panic
that the children might
find out they are frauds.

The main problem being
the way the human body
refuses to be thoroughly
understood by science...

why that second opinion
often sounds to us as if
the first one had no idea
what it was talking about.

That is why the hallways
in hospitals are so straight,
and the doors evenly spaced.
We need something to trust.

But... even when their best
is not enough, doctors still
often offer us much more
than we would've gotten

from our Aunt Dorothy
or that one creepy lady
at the end of the street
with a book of spells.

Unless... it turns out,
in the end, creepy lady
does have the answers
to what ails us, after all,

which's when we begin
to fathom that healing
requires a calmed head,
and a hard-willed heart—

and some amount of belief,
to go with a good doctor's
education, and the lady's
book of creepy spells.

Categories

> ~ for Brian Franklin
> (and Rumpelstiltskin)
> Sunday, April 5

"Not a Chance in Hell"
is an actual coronavirus
category—according to
one of my oldest friends
—and, I only have two
left in that category—

who waits on steel pins
and carbon needles for
a new, or a used, heart
and decent set of lungs
in this time of almost
certain impossibilities.

He is my age, and yet,
he shares that category
with my dad, dear God,
please, help them both.

And, because of him,
and them, and others,
I've had to crawl back
in a cave of no-news…

news that sounds like
sand in an hourglass.

So I just huddle up,
head down, building
fires by rubbing sticks,
boiling up a rabbit stew
above the primal flame,

and then hopping about
in the flickering of light,
singing,
> *The queen will*
> *never win the game...*
> *for Rumpelstiltskin*
> *is my name...*

Which, I suppose,
puts me in some
sort of other
category.

Deep Thought,
and Other Supercomputers

~ for Dave Charlson
April 6, 2020

There'll be 24 hours
in each of the 24 days
left in the days of April.

And in the 24 minutes
it's taken me to write
these few lines so far,

I have thought about
the number on Jeff
Gordon's stock car,

Kobe Bryant's jersey,
or... Four-and-Twenty
at the Hollywood Derby.

It is the number of carats
in pure gold, and the cycles
of the Chinese Solar Year...

also the number of chapters
in the *Odyssey*... and points
on a backgammon board.

By the way… it was one
of my six lucky numbers
in today's fortune cookie.

It is, also, twice as many
as the Twelve Tribes of
the Nation of Israel, but…

mysteriously… it happens to be
the Answer to the Ultimate Question
of Life, the Universe, and Everything…

backwards.   Oooo…
At least according to Deep Thought
in Adams's Guide to the Galaxy.

Anyway, I'm beginning to see
the eerie side-effects of stay-
at-home—as I catch myself

counting the slow minutes
in every 24-hour day…
which I worry I may

catch myself doing
for each of the next
four-and-twenty days.

Social Distancing

> ~ for Jeanne Fell
> Monday, April 6

My name, in Hebrew,
means "Gift of God."
I recall the big eye-rolls
of my two older brothers.
I learned to play by myself.

I remember the girls—those
radiant creatures who walked
a wide berth around me—back
in the dark halls of middle school.

And I'm not sure I ever went to one
football game in my high school days.
I preferred the idea of jungles, knives,
animals, and Jane swinging on vines.

In my 20s—that golden decade
of guitars and synthesizers—
I wrote songs with guys who
had names like Blade, Uncle
Dave, and ol' Sergio Gypsy…
the last two being the same guy.

Even now, friends are mostly a thing
my wife feels I should have more of.

When I squat at the bar in Maria's
in Santa Fe, I'll pull out a journal
and write sonnets to margaritas.
That way, I can always count on
the stool next to me staying empty.

I like to buy my limes, coffee, cheese,
and ibuprofen in the evening hours,
when I know everyone else here
is at home watching reality TV.

I was born in East Texas, raised
in the heart of Oklahoma, and now
I live in the Hill Country of Texas…
and believe Trump's the Grim Reaper.

I also have a sneaking suspicion that
God does not give a damn about
the U.S. economy. So, honestly,
for me? … Social distancing?
Just a year like any other.

SLOUCHING TOWARDS HEAVEN

~ for Kenneth Copeland
Tuesday, April 7

There are killers among us
this sunny Sunday morning,
their hands clasped, white-
knuckled in sick devotion
and a sanctified denial.

They pray for our souls,
that we will be saved, or,
if not, then swiftly relieved
of our breath and disgrace.

And, these killers among us
will soon be leaving churches
in Texas and Louisiana and all
through the bursting Bible Belt,
headed for the nearest Applebee's.

Though curbside is all they can get,
they've gotta have their deep-fried
dogma before hitting the streets
to spread the gospel, and germs.

Fort Worth's Kenneth Copeland,
himself, has mega-tel-evangelized

blowing "the wind of God" into
the face of Satan's demon-virus,
that his followers can be healed
of it by touching their screens,
just be sure to keep those tithes
and offerings flowing in, Amen?

My guess is that he'll experience
an 80% success rate… in fleecing
his flock into writing those checks,
hopefully before they're hospitalized.

Yes, he pursed and puckered those
made-up lips, like he was ready
for a holy phallus, and blew,
right into the camera lens.

She Calls It Prayer

~ for Norma Brown
Wednesday, April 8

Mom...
like Anne Lamott...
has a serious case of *grippage*.

She's held on for the dear lives
of her loved ones, for as long
as any of them can remember.

But she may've met her match
in this novel coronavirus—yes,
not even her exceptional powers

of worry are enough to control
a worldwide pandemic. And
she is a bit baffled by it...

she's always been able to light
candles in her studio and worry
all of us through illness and failure.

There's gotta be some other side,
and with enough concern, she
can will us over and into it.

I've not been smart enough
to be more grateful for this love,
which is what grippage ultimately is.

But now, with kids, grandchildren,
and relatives all over the red map,
she's realizing that all she can do

is put the kettle on, thoughtfully
spoon out the English breakfast
tea, and yes, still light the candles.

Dad will need his scrambled egg,
and to be reminded when it's time
to take his pills before each meal.

So… she's doing her best to leave
the room when the news comes on,
and to just… not… think about it.

WHAT NOT

~ for Lavonn Brown
Wednesday, April 8

My dad wants me
to write his eulogy
now,
    so he can edit it
before he comes down
with symptoms or anything
else that threatens those men
born into the Silent Generation.

I am trying to laugh at his joke,
which may or may not be one,
but I can see the sense in it.

How nice to have control
over what need not be said.
And I can tell you that's likely
to be his chief concern about it.

The man delivered thousands…
as a preacher for over 55 years.
So, he has a powerful sense
for what simply does not
matter in the end.

Shelter-in-Place

> ~ for Betty Potts
> Thursday, April 9

> Come in, she said, I'll give ya
> shelter from the storm.
> ~ Bob Dylan

I grew up sheltered-in-life.
The third son of a preacher,
with a mother who sacrificed
her dreams for the different
dreams of her very different
three boys, in what I'd call
a middle class family, living
in a city of just over a hundred
thousand smack dab in the middle
of Oklahoma, one of two states
that claim to be the middle of
the United States. Norman
was a nearly-perfect place
to go from kindergarten
through the 12th grade
having absolutely no
idea that the other 99%
of the world's population
didn't live in the same fairly
safe, trouble-free conditions.

So I played, sheltered-in-mind,
in the elms of the schoolyard.
I'd climb, sit, think for hours
on end. Or, in the backyard,
we'd shoot off firecrackers
whatever the time of year.
On the streets, after dark,
we'd ride our bikes because
no driver was on a cellphone.

I am now sheltered-in-heart.
Even though I lost a few
decades to bad loves,
I have found a wife
who's sheltered me
in peace and healing
until I began, slowly,
to come back to myself.

No matter what some may
think, I'm sheltered-in-hope
because I owe my daughter
and her generation more
than a carefully-honed
sense of cynicism.

So to be told to
shelter-in-place,
for fellow citizens,
in an uncertain time,
does not bother me.

Oxford's absurdly big
dictionary says the word
shelter is of uncertain origin,
possibly having to do with the
Old English: "sćieldtruma,"
where we likely got "shield."

But the word now means…
a structure giving protection
from, among many things,

rain, wind, or sun; danger,
attack; a place of safety,
giving protection from
air raids, nuclear fallout;
refuge for the homeless,
and also the oppressed.

And I'm just sayin'…
sounds good to me.

WHAT I SHOULD REALLY TELL MY
  THERAPIST IS:

~ for Tim Zeddies
Friday, April 10

Session I

I told you so.

Please leave a little neurosis in there,
for good measure. I need it for work.

Quarantine? I've felt this all my life.

Stay-at-home? All I've ever wanted.

Shelter-in-place? Man... I can do that
with a thousand people in the audience.

We should've listened to Chicken Little.

I am not, necessarily, wrong about her,
and him. Nor the other hers and hims.

You know I'm analyzing you too.

I have secret powers.

I have not told you everything.
Not even in this prolix poem.

Just because I am a cynic,
doesn't mean the world
is not full of shit.

I believe in poetic justice…
I believe one of its better sentences
would be served by President #45
spending a couple of weeks in ICU
on a ventilator he has to share
with a bisexual bus driver
who's now lost his job
and health insurance.

Now whether or not
its greatest sentence
would be carried out…
well that'd be up to God.

I acknowledge the evil in me.
It's how I locate the good in me.

If a picture paints a thousand words,
then I will write two thousand…
and, so, kick the picture's ass.

That which does not kill us,
makes us age...   terribly.

On the poetry shelf at the bookstore,
there is something for everyone.
But, I am always amazed
at how much of it is
for someone else.

Humor, often dark,
sometimes even sick,
is the only way I can deal
with the tragedy and sorrow.
Let alone the lunatics all around.

No matter how artfully you say something,
it can never cover for having nothing to say.

The written, spoken, and performed arts
will die without a revolution of silence.

My writing practice, so far, has been
a very careful, and steady, violation
of most critics' personal preferences.

The last seven or eight pithy little quotes
give you a hint of the signal to noise ratio

in my head during any given hour or so.

Hey… are you writing all this down?

And so how does all this make *you* feel?

Have you heard of the Midnight Disease?

This will be the longest poem
in an already long book.

Are you sorry yet?

I wasn't raised to not trust
just about everyone. Just about
everyone over the last five decades,
eventually, helped me to get there.

I like burning shit. Candles, fires,
bad books of poetry, and stuff.

I'm not afraid of the coronavirus.
Actually it's quite nice for a change
to know that there is absolutely
nothing else I should be doing.

At the grocery store these days,
it's never been easier to spot
the sociopathic egomaniacs
with a sudden new interest
in the practice of eugenics.

I love Vienna Sausages, and
ice cream with toffee bits in it.

I've been thinking too much
about what I'd do if, suddenly,
my diet wasn't going to add a day.

I love my country, but I am getting
pretty damn tired of its united states.

I appreciate your efforts to save us…
but, not all of us are worth the grief.

So what are all the things my wife has
come in here and told you about me?

We should have been recording us…
you know, for my university archives.
They love this kind of viscous bullshit.
Especially those hacksaw biographers.

Can you see an end to my troubles?

I never had full-on intercourse
until I was 24… give or take.

Maybe that's where we should
start: the beginning of all this.

God, how I do love sex.

Nooow I think we're
getting somewhere.

I'm sorry, we've run out of time
for today, but I'll be back soon.

Session II

Where did we leave off?

Ah… yes… sex, I think it was.

Did I mention how much I love it?

You know? One of these days, when
I, at long last, am totally patched up,

you and I… we're gonna toss back
a few of my ass-knock margaritas
out around my ass-kick fire pit,
and *you* are going to tell *me*
a thing or two. Alright?

You strike me as someone
who could use a little help too.

And I don't charge near as much.

I think ol' Sigmund was right,
as well as those others who
came after and discounted
his somber Oedipal theories.

I also think the Tiger King has a point.

Understand… I have nothing else
to do for the next few months.
And this is really helping me.

You know, that if anything
happens to mom and dad
as a result of this disease
and the President picking
toilet paper out of his ass,

the two of us'll be seeing
a lot more of each other.

More people have more time
to break out the leaf blowers now.
Another reason we'll need to talk soon.

Conservative psycho-religious republican
types offer an endless source of inspiration.
Without them, my well would surely run dry.
That ever-presence of God's antithesis
reminds me to keep the faith that
I keep joking I had to let go.

It never ceases to shock me
when people take me seriously.

Do you ever fake listening?

Don't feel bad.
I do it for a living too.

My neighbor across the street
is mowing his lawn. But I like him.
He came from the Upper Peninsula.
No bullshit with people who put up
with winters like that. He also works

at a liquor store—so, we exchange
money for tequila on the porch.
Therefore, we maintain
a relative stasis.
And, I respect
whiskey drinkers.

I think people who have
never read a book of poetry
should not be allowed to vote.

I think people who send in poems
to *The New Yorker*, shouldn't either.

I believe the monsters who do dark
and truly terrible things to children
should be chained to a cliff face
with their eyes stapled open,
so they'll have to watch
those vultures land
to do their thing.

I believe oak trees
are fully conscious.

I know crazy, old, drunk,
Japanese philosopher-hermits

who agree with me 100 percent.

I think Bukowski lied about a lot
of things, and yet still managed
to be right about most of it.

Every morning I say to myself,
This could be the day I go
without a margarita.

I am nothing but
a meager vagabond
with books in the trunk
and guitars in the backseat,
and I have a gorgeous wife,
and a fabulous home, here
in the hills of central Texas.

Yep, I can't believe it either.

What? Our time's up again?

Session III

Anyway... where were we?

Ah... yes... vagabond poet.

A great songwriter, John Gorka,
put this phrase in a song one time:

> People love you when they
> know you're leaving soon.

(I don't know where he got it.
But we all steal the good stuff.)

That line ties in, notably, with
the gorgeous wife thing as well.

I challenged a guy to a duel once.

I have also noticed people love me
more when I write, instead of talk.
It allows them to maintain a safer
distance from my more peculiar
and often disturbing thoughts.

I've thought about leaving.
Not her… just everything.

I get nervous every time
you write something down.

I sometimes take long walks
between these little stanzas.

Isn't it… just… okay…
to just… sometimes…
be depressed for a while?

What would your diagnosis be
if I never came out of quarantine?

I have a friend who can't say where
he is, for security purposes—except
that he's trapped inside 20-foot walls
somewhere in the desert dustbin of
the Saudi Arabian wilderness. So,
how do we define that isolation?

I miss my life out on the road
that I have grown so tired of.

Therapy is hard on me, since
it forces me to think too much
about what I do all the time…
which is… to think too much.

For a long time… I did not
believe in what it is you do.

For a long time, I believed
God would take care of it.
But, eventually, I had to
terminate our contract
on religious grounds.

Since then, however,
our relationship has
taken a serious turn
for the better. But,
I think I've already
talked about that?

I hate people who
tell the same joke
again and again
at every party.

And look… if
you've already read
this far, I might as well
go ahead and get it all out.

I harmed my daughter, by not
digging through this stuff earlier.

Self-forgiveness for that will be
a long, and a hard-fought, battle.

I'm looking for something in those
stones I stack all over the place…
I just don't know what it is yet.
But, I'll be sure to fill you in.

Man, one o' these Augusts,
I am going to flip Texas
the bird and never live
through another one
here again—not ever.

Religion is the real virus,
politics its snake-oil cure.

They are coming for me.

I don't believe it's all me.

I once drank a bona fide
Mexican cowboy under
his own table, to the tune
of his own 100-dollar bottle
of Don Julio 1942 Tequila.

Unfailing goodness, eternal
grace, and indiscriminate mercy
can be their own form of tyranny.

Absolute equality, at its deepest
linguistic root, is unachievable
and would be terribly boring.

I have my own scales
for measuring.

One of the things
I said in this session
was a complete lie.

Sometimes, a lie
is simply a better
version of a story.

My mother once said
I had the Mark of Cain,
since the day I was born.

So... what did we think
we'd accomplish here?

Besides, like I said
early on, I haven't
told you everything.
Not even in this poem.

On the Rebound

~ for Susie Clevenger
Saturday, April 11

She never had a dime…
because she gave each one
away to those she believed
needed it more. Her faith
in life to do the right thing
was so much stronger than
the bonds of limited funds.
The end comes, and voilà,
Y' see? It did not matter.

It is hard to live freer.
And now, everyone
is having to decide
if she was right.

The entire world,
minus the wealthy
landlords, is having
to look into pantries
and wallets and run new
calculations and algorithms
on what we're surprised to find
we can, it seems, live without now.

If there's no toilet paper on the shelves,
there is no toilet paper on the shelves.
And squatting down to think about it
real hard, ain't gonna make it appear.

So it is that the survivors among us
who'll thrive quicker than the rest
are the empty-pocket optimists,

those who never did need it
to begin with.

Again, for the First Time

> ~ for Sierra Brown
> Monday, April 13

I saw a dog out walking
its two pets this morning
as if it had never been
on a walk before…
nose down deep
in some weed,
wiggling, flaring,
as if that thing was
nature porn, and green
the tint and hue of ecstasy.

She turned her nostrils up
to them as if to yelp, "Oh.
My. God! Have you *smelled*
anything like this in your sad
little human lives? Come. On!"
But, they did not notice her,
because they were too busy
gawking up at the sky as if
they had never seen a sky,
or the color of blue, ever.
Hands shading their eyes.

So... she jerked them on
to the next glorious weed.
Tail wagging in an almost
unconscious doggish joy.
And they took joy in hers.
Laughing and talking as if
they'd forgotten this joy.
The joy of no deadlines,
nor any business dinner
or boring cocktail thing
they will need to shower
and be dressed for by 5:15,
because being forced to stay
at home finally forced them
up off their duffs and outside,
where they're seeing and hearing
birds they don't recall the names of,
smelling the jasmine vines that they
can't remember either, so they snap
fingers above heads in the question,
What is it those things are called again?

And the dog rolled its eyes...
heaving onward, leading
with its furious nose,
spoiled, now...
forever.

BACK TO WHAT?

~ for Miriam Rieck
Tuesday, April 14

He kind of misses the sound
of the copy machine. The one
near the breakroom, where she
pretends to pay him no attention
when he creates a bogus excuse
to happen, y' know, to walk by.

She longs for the small masses
of people on South Congress
as she sips on her triple shot
at the sidewalk table at Jo's
and flips through Instagram,
searching for all those hearts
that beat and glow red there,
while the odd, the sad, and
the zany, go parading by.

He wants back the hour
and twenty minutes of
relative peace and NPR
on a morning commute.

She just... dear God...
wants him... to please

get out of the house.
And for their kids...
dear... sweet Jesus,
Lord and Savior...
to return to school.
It is the only chance
she'll ever love them
again, in the future.

He has got to have
that barstool back.
The one at the far
end, in The Shed?
He drinks too fast
from his own bottle.

She lost her job pre-
pandemic...   so...
no need to hasten
back to anything like
normal on her account.

The city streets, buildings,
and the grocery store aisles
felt like zombietown to him
before all the undead started
wearing facemasks and gloves.

From Rancho Cucamonga in L.A.,
she can see 40 miles to Mt. Jacinto
out in Palm Springs. She cannot
remember the last time...

Here on Lake Sakakawea,
in the west of North Dakota,
he only recently heard the news
somethin's 'goin' on' in the world.

She knows it's over between them.
So, there is nothing to return to.

These two've simply decided
to never leave home again.
The sex is too good...

One, at Least

~ for Trina Kopacka
Wednesday, April 15

She remembers
a slight kindness
I paid 42 years ago.

I was a better person
in the seventh grade.

She says she fell off
the pommel horse
in gym class. And,
instead of laughing,
I came over to help
her get on her feet.

She says Longfellow
Middle School was
a time and a place
chock-full of jerks
smirking in the halls.

And I think, Okay now
we're getting somewhere.
It's all coming back to me.

The days of our terror,
and yet, determination.

The horrendous desire
to belong… to fit in…
while feeling nauseous
at whiffs of the cesspit
we were trying to fit into.

In better cultures, the rites
of passage are more clearly
defined and well planned out.

Here in the Land of Oz, though,
it's mayhem, and we get no wise
old shaman to lead us through.

It's pommel horses, jerkwads,
and that damned thick rope
we can never quite climb
all the way to the top.

So I'm pleased I had one
good moment in life, at least.

Honor Thy Mother

~ for Nancy Walasky
Friday, April 17

Oh, Madre Naturaleza…
Ay la madre, nuestra madre
of the one and holy Earth…

she has awakened in the fog
of one hellacious hangover,
rubbed her all-seeing eyes,

and she is not happy, friends.
She'd thought she could doze
while all the children played.

Big mistake, she thought,
as she looked at the place
and the way we'd left it.

"Ay dios," began as a low
rumble in her volcanic throat,
before erupting in profane lava.

So she reached up to straighten
la corona, that golden crown,
but instead, she removed it.

She paused, thought first
about the consequences,
and then, in her terrifying

love, cast down esa corona.
It rolled around and through
the partying, polluting nations,

lightning hissing into every dark
and grubby corner of our neglect,
our refusal to guard her treasure.

And we, the wayward children,
all the guilty hijas y hijos, yes,
we see, now, what it means

to dishonor the Mother
of the trees and stones,
and all that has breath.

Too Quiet

> ~ Christa Bolain
> Saturday, April 18

It's a thing we think
we are missing in life,
until it is lowered down
over us like a big biodome.
Now the silences and stillness
brood around and over us as if
we are stuck in a house full
of cats that we cannot
go buy food for.
And when they lose
their humor and patience,
the scene could get pretty ugly.
So, we pet them and try to recall
the last time circumstances left us
alone with our thoughts for some
undetermined number of months.

Most of us realizing that's never
happened before, we pause…
in a wondrous sense of fear,
put the pen down for a time…
and in a fearful sense of wonder,
we wonder how long we can go
before we begin having it out

with the apparition of a striped
cat with a huge toothy grin who
won't stop singing the first verse
of Jabberwocky. It ain't no joke.
So, we crack the front window
and notice the weird volumes
of birds twittering in bushes
and a recycling truck, three
blocks over, juggling plastic
and breaking liquor bottles.

And the dog, asleep, snoring
on the bed, dreams of nothing
new. This quiet day will be like
any other. Only humans could
make this wondrous serenity
both a blessing and a curse.
Which doesn't help us...
thank you very much.

And, for a few seconds,
we may consider reasoning
with the condescending dog.

But we stop short, because
we're afraid she's right.

WIRELESS

> ~ for Luri Owen
> Sunday, April 19

Dad came from the generation
that refused what computers
had to offer. Writing checks,
using cash, those were ways
to see where money went
and how little was left…
the mail always delivered
the monthly news of how
much electricity had been
wasted by our excesses…
the reason a newfangledy
television remote control
was about as far as this ol'
fogey was willing to go in
the realm of technology.
And, he'd only use four
or five of its 37 buttons.
So, when her cellphone,
    all those miles away,
began to die, she knew
there was about to be
a horrible silence…
that he would not
understand.

Phantom Opera

~ for Karen Tardiff
Monday, April 20

East of here, tornados
just destroyed neighborhoods
where families tried to quarantine,
but now just stand with their houses
down around their ankles, and no one
can find their masks or hand sanitizer.

West and a little north of here, snow
has friends of mine rubbing heads
and querying if germs can travel
on flakes blowing at 50 mph.

Here in the hills of Texas,
these last couple of days
have been what some
Texans think is cold.

Yet today, of course,
our thermometer reads
a more springy 90 degrees.

But who are we to complain?
In Kenya? 200 billion locusts
are eating their weight in crops

while swarming the continent
because, many scientists said,
of heavy rains that have fallen
way out in the Arabian desert.

So it is that nature seems to be
singing in a chorus of voices…
not just the viral tenor of death.

The bass of winds gone wild,
the soprano of belated snow,
and the baritone of insects,
who will, for the record,
someday rule the world,

they are performing an opera
we have no choice but to attend.

The Last Haboob

> ~ for Christopher Brooks
> Tuesday, April 21

You spoke of absences,

> the obtrusive contrails
> that incarcerate the Arabian
> wilderness sky, like barbed
> wire across the prairie.

You explained how when
"they aren't there, the mail
doesn't run." So I'll not kid
myself, or you, or anyone into
thinking *I'm* writing *you* a poem.

> I've had to jump from bed
> to floor a few times, courtesy of
> Houthi rebel missiles from Yemen.

It seems sometime back in the 1950s
the poets forgot what it was that
the truth is stranger than…
and they have long since
suffered the anonymity
of such a sad denial.

Even now, they continue
to believe a life not lived
can be made interesting.

So when you write to me,

> this ancient caravan place,
> as barren as the lunar surface,

or how you washed your lips

> with bootleg bourbon
> and pipe smoke, my
> desert perfumes,

I hate to think how little
attention those poets'll pay.

Still, you are a pretty tough guy
doing a damned tough job under
some damned tough circumstances
trapped inside four high walls where

> every day it's hard to breathe
> with all the blowing dust,

and you're scraping together
meals of commissary rations,

> roasted Cornish game hen
> with fresh rosemary and lemon.

And so I doubt those literary dorks
will cause you to lose much sleep.
You have rebel missiles for that.

Besides, you also told me
that almost all of your

> western fears and stereotypes
> blew away with the last haboob.

But, especially after that enigmatic
Saudi woman you met, the one with

> a delicate neck painted in birds,

the one with the necklace of bone who,

> from within her niqab, she speaks
> to me about gratitude, how she
> is grateful to breathe every day.

So, I thank you for condescending
to have me write a piece for you.
And thank you, even more, for
doing all of the work for me.

You, with your Bangladeshi
friend on his bicycle. And you,
with the Pakistanis who watered
"the palms and bougainvillea with
a big tanker truck." You, who even
spelled "bougainvillea" correctly.

And you, living with the recent
absence of the green parrots.

Yes...   you...
are the poet...
my friend.

Earth Day

> Wednesday, April 22

We gave the Earth a birthday,
assigned since we have no record.

When your parents are gas and dust
swirling, who came together only
because of gravity, and not for
any feeling, then, of course,
you'll be left with a deep
and volcanic burning
in your central core
and rocky mantle.

Essentially orphaned,
some 93 million miles away
from the nearest source of light,
she raised us without any guidance,
giving us food, water, and shelter.

And, like any spoiled and rotten
little brats, we'd never considered
how she might grow so old and tired,
she could no longer take care of herself.

And, like all sets of contentious siblings,
some of us will care more than others.

And those of us who do—we
who care the most—we'll try
to keep sheets changed, and
the bedpan good and clean.

We'll want to be by her side,
holding her withered hands.

And yet… while we watch,
wait, listen in for breathing,
we'll look around, nervously,
at each other towards the end,

wondering where, in the world,
we're going to spread her ashes.

A Strange Gap

> ~ for Kayla Anderson
> Thursday, April 23

To stay six feet away
from the ones we love,
masks hiding our smiles,
no permission to close that
preposterously small distance
and move on in for a hug, that's
a very different kind of longing.

In times of war we have seven
continents to contain our fear
and desperation, 10,000 miles
to diffuse the heavy ordnance
of our deep, relentless worry.
But quarantine allows for us
to look straight into the eyes
of those we're afraid to lose
to nature's indiscriminations.
There is a unique cruelty to it.
We can't find our bearings. So,
we sit, and stare, back and forth,
in dumbfoundedness. And we wait,
counting the days and feet between us.

Stepping Out

> ~ for Treg Isaacson
> Friday, April 24

> In the middle of the road of our life
> I awoke in a dark wood,
> Where the true way was wholly lost
>
> ~ Dante Alighieri, *The Inferno*

There's a trail… a path…
almost always some way…
no matter how dark, or how
deep, those woods may appear.

There's an easing of the thickness
that leads to another easing—often
just beyond the muted, fallen sadness
of a great thing long ago sawed down.

And you'll recognize the greatness of it
by the new life that sprouted all around,
and even straight from, its ancient core,
as it remains dignified in its decaying.

More than you can say for the one
who cut it down and left it there,
off to find some other beauty
to destroy with a huge blade.

But Frost and Dante both
taught us how a way leads
onto another way—even if
we have to pass through hell.

The trick is in the first step…
the one we often don't want
to take, as we pause a while
to go over the supply list.

But, the Earth is known
to nourish travelers in odd
and unexpected ways—when
we step in respect and gratitude.

Just a Visitor Here

~ for Denny McCoy
Friday, April 24

To say there was no one else
present to witness the thing,
is to say there was no one else
present to witness that it didn't.
Which only makes the question
more difficult: So… if a poet
goes for a walk in the forest
and falls, can we trust him?

I took a walk, nonetheless.
And it was in a damn forest.
So, you'll have to decide now
if indeed you want to read on.
But I am telling you, halfway in
I found myself in a dark wood—
my way not wholly lost, not yet—
suddenly, face to face with a hare.

Do you know a female hare is a Jill?
And, get this, that the male is a Jack?
But she just stood there, munching
on a sweet little weed, unstartled.
And, with a mouthful she said,
in a voice like Jessica Rabbit's,

with a touch of Mae West maybe,
"So how goes it in the holy hovels
and dim-lit dens of humans, there
in the clutches of such a demise?"

I said, "What?" half out of shock,
half for her impressive eloquence.

"Having a little trouble with, might
we say, the equivocacies of nature
these days in Never-never land?"

Still rattled, I said "What?" again.
And recalling my vocation as poet,
I chastised myself for not offering
more pithy responses. But, jiminy!
What's up with the animals lately?

Unimpressed, she licked her lips
and went back for some more
of that sweet weed the Earth
provides for free. That part,
she did not say, I just sort of
figured it out. Then she said,
in a normal tone, "And so…
you're good on toilet paper."

"Yes," I said, happy that I came
up with something besides *what*
this time, and feeling a bit smug
that I'd recently scored some TP.

"Humans bewilder us with every
thing they deem to be a necessity.
And it's not lost on us, by the way,
why September's so much hotter."

I could see where this was going…
and all six of her points were sharp.
So I took good care not to add on,
nor to stack the deck in her favor.

Yeah, there comes a time in very
few men's lives when they must
admit to being bested by a hare.

I did not have a rifle with me,
our typical refuge. Therefore,
I tipped my hat to acquiesce.

Involunteer

> ~ for Daniella DeLaRue
> Saturday, April 25

To speak of keeping distances,
5,000 miles, plus some, mostly
over a deep ocean, would seem
sufficient to the cause of isolation.

She felt safe, mangos and papayas
grew in the backyard—bananas,
pineapple, coconuts never out
of reach. Toilet paper, plenty.

Local friends, sweet as island
fruit. The temperature, seldom
above 90°, very rarely below 80.
Hibiscus and the Pandanus Palms.

All the shrimp and crab she can eat.
Clownfish and coral, the cuckoos,
and even the occasional flying fox.
It's life by waves of the South Pacific.

So when the orders came, behind news
of the virus, she had just hours to pack.
Hours to decide what mattered. Socks,
or mangos… blue jeans, or a papaya?

Who to say goodbye to? How many?
She'd be returning, right? What the
hell... and... whose idea was this?
Always someone in Washington.

And there you have it. It's back
to Port Arthur, Texas. Where
it will, soon enough, be 110°
beating on the oil refineries.

So, just after liftoff, there was
little to do but cry for the peace
she'd felt in serving the Corps...
and look, for as long as she could,

out the window... and back at...
the Tongan and American flags
fluttering in the hands of friends,
as she whispered... *Ofa lahi atu...*

> *I love you so much.*

CLIFFHANGER

~ for Lise Liddell
Sunday, April 26

In her days as a banker,
she ran herself just this side
of death. And that's no metaphor.
We're talking six to ten miles every
morning before work—which led
to crazy runner types talking her
into training for marathons next.

That's not to say that a metaphor
didn't exist in the passing shadows.
All that "away from" kind of stuff,
as opposed to "to something"...
you know... that stuff we go
to therapy for for 20 years.

But, when her knees, lower
back, and everything else that
hurt like hell, forced her to quit,
the banking as well as the running,
she poured her time into her guitar,
which she did well, and also helping
others—which she also did, very well.
Too well, as not all of them deserved it.

And so, with a soul on the brink
of losing its balance, these months
of intentional seclusion, in cahoots
with an angel sipping chardonnay,
led her to a small cabin in the hills
of Texas where her vocation now
is creating novel cocktail recipes,
inventing new ways to eat cheese,
things she's deciding matter more.

And as she lounges by the sunsets,
sipping and nibbling, then nibbling
and sipping, she's taken to musing
over the words of her heroines...

Mae West, "When I'm good,
I'm very good. But when
I'm bad... I'm better."

Or her mother quipping,
"I pride myself on having
taught my children how
to properly cuss."

She takes solace
in Barbara Streisand
divulging if not imploring,

"Oh God, don't envy me,
I have my own pains."

And in Lucille Ball saying,
"I'd rather regret the things
I have done than the things
that I haven't." (Mic drop.)

And she knows that a force
grows inside the collective
lives of powerful women.

And she's beginning to see
the long string of evidence
of the same within her own.

She feels a never-too-lateness
welling up in her eyes and bones.

She's thinking now about making
some damn-straight changes too.

So, for all of her possibly-friends,
but especially all of the maybe-men,
in her near, rapidly-reclaiming future,
she would like for you to also know

she's been thinking about the line
from *Thelma and Louise*, the one
Louise lays down, just seconds
after blowing away that rapist,

"You watch your mouth, buddy."

MORE THAN YOUR PARENTS
WANT ME TO SAY

~ for Matthew McQuistion, on turning 18
Monday, April 27

Alexander the Great
was already conquering
most of the Mediterranean
at the ripe ol' age of eighteen.
Yet... he burned out, big-time,
and died of a simple fever at 32.
So let's not use him as an example.

Joan of Arc, at only seventeen,
chopped off her hair, started
wearing men's clothes, and
altered the very course of
the Hundred Years' War
by kicking some serious
English ass. Thing is...
she was captured about
two years later... and...
then burned at the stake.

My God, Greta Thunberg
was born in January of 2003,
and she already has the power to

send the leader of the United States
into episodic psycho-tweeting seizures.

But none of these notable deeds
overshadow how crazy it is
to still be classified as
a *teenager*, and yet
demonstrating
clear-cut proof
that you are more
intelligent and stable
than the sad majority of
the voting population here
in the country of your birth.

And I wish I could help you.
But I don't have any answers.
I used to, back in, say, my 20s,
but I lost them when I hit my 40s.

Here is what little I have figured out.

For one, that whole guitar, let's-make-
a-band, rock-star thing is a great big lie.
The music biz was one of the toughest
jobs I've ever had. It's worse than any
reality TV show they've made about it.

And groupies do not make for healthy
girlfriends. Or... much worse... wives.
If you choose the arts, no matter which,
you must love "it" for the sake of "it."

Two, money no longer holds the comfy
promises it once might have. Though,
I doubt that it ever did. King Herod
died grossly obese, and miserable,
in a pile of gold and emeralds.
So, few things have served
to make me happier than
finally coming to terms
with what is "enough."

And last, because I'm sure
my time expired minutes ago,
nothing impacted my life more
than learning the tricks and trade,
the power and punch, of words.

So, best of luck to you...
and good wishes...

                Nathan

Quarantoonie

> ~ for Stephen Lawson
> Tuesday, April 28

I experienced three mornings
the other day. I know… weird.
And I always look up the word
"weird," because I can never
remember whether the "e"
does in fact go before "i."
The same way I always
have to look up "wield"
to make sure that the "i"
falls first. Drives me nuts.
Anyway, so, the other day?
I made coffee, toasted toast,
went to our library, lit a candle,
and wrote a damn poem… three
times. Yes, three times in one day.
Morning, afternoon, and then again
in the afternoon, only a little later.
I know people who are leaning
on their kitchen counters and
counting a strawberry's seeds.
One girl, she is alphabetizing
more than a thousand books
she has not read, but refuses
to ever get rid of, just in case.

And, this one guy? He is now
building a sort of shrine thing
out of emptied tequila bottles
that seem to keep appearing?
Ashley recently came outside,
because she had not seen me
for hours, to find me sitting
on the very hard ground over
in our extra lot as I picked up
one small stone at a time and
placed it in a rusty metal pail.
And, just then, I had to stop
and chew on the difference
between "pail" and "pale,"
so I'd use the correct term.
I'm even looking up words
like "toonie" for reasons
I can't put a finger on.
It's a Canadian coin
worth two dollars.
Sort of like the way
I'm making up words
like quarantoonie, then
trying to decide if it's
a noun? Or a verb?
Maybe adjective?

IF YOU CARE

                    Tuesday, April 28

Look, I don't care
that you don't care.
However, be aware
how much I do care
how much you also
seem to not care that
there are other people
who do care about this.

Also, please be aware,
or do I mean beware,
that I am highly aware
of the fine point where
your not caring slips into
the dark realm of uncaring.

Are you aware of that subtle
difference, critical in the sense
that uncaring is an offence,
where not caring is more
or less indifference?

So, be aware as well
that if your not caring
becomes more and more

uncaring, my care will
become, more and more,
caring, critical in the sense
that I may slip into the dark
realm of taking big offence
to your selfish indifference,

and no amount of bewaring
will do any amount of
preparing you for
just how intense
my taking offence
may then become,
critical in the sense
that you may suddenly
sense that there is, in fact,
something you very much do…

                                                    care about.

Well, Hello

> ~ for Bob Wood
> Wednesday, April 29

My least favorite greeting
is the limp handshake
at a cocktail party
that, inevitably,
entails the shak-er
looking over a shoulder
of the shak-ee for anyone
who may be more important.

It's an extraordinary way
to, truly, not be seen.

And it has me thinking
about how I do not miss
this manual custom handed
down, through 2,500 years,
of not trusting the person
who stands before you.

Designed as a sly means
to check a man for weapons—
make sure there's no knife hidden
up a sleeve below his steely grin—

shaking hands symbolizes
the "suspect" in us all.

And so it is that, now,
in its socially prescribed
absence, we are forced to,
once again, look each other

                in the eyes.

YES, HELLO

> ~ for Bob Wood
> Wednesday, April 29

If we want to root ourselves
in a more honorable way
to greet one another…

we could reach back
beyond the Greeks
and their suspicions,
disguised in a gesture
of peace and good will,
to the ancient tongue
of Sanskrit, with its
palms pressed and
fingers pointing up.

And from a respectable
distance, we could offer
to salute the divine within
the pilgrim across from us.

Imagine the consciousness.

Imagine the unmistakable
intent in such a message.

Imagine how much tougher
it would be to lie to someone.

And just imagine all the germs
that would never leave home.

And much like the germs…
imagine how uncomfortable
it would make the blue suits
and red ties on Capitol Hill,
how difficult it would make
doing business as usual there.

Imagine how their pallid faces
and tattooed grimaces would
contort as they try to form
those foreign syllables,

"Na-ma-ste"

LUCKY?

~ for Roz Nevin Tyburski
Thursday, April 30

It's a tough time to be lucky.
Whatever lucky may mean
to whoever claims it.

Long ago, it served
as a title that preceded
the proper name of a lady
who owned her own alehouse.

Another antiquated definition was
"An act of escaping; a getaway."
You actually "Made a lucky."

For some a four-leaf clover.
For others a favorite cereal.

With steely eyes squinted,
Clint Eastwood asked us
if we were sure we felt it?

Now, more than ever before,
it means you are able to work
on a laptop at a kitchen table.

Which means, among other
delicate and difficult things,
you do not have to stand, or
sit in your car, in a four-hour
line to be denied free dry goods
since you were three too deep.

So who do you tell, off-mic,
that you miss your daughter
because of an invisible line
drawn in the invisible sand.

Despite the good reasons,
the sorrow eats like acid,
and what it means to be
lucky is redefined again.

Is it lucky to get to see
him one last time, even
if through panes of glass?

Is it lucky to have already
chosen a simplified life
of relative seclusion
in the Texas Hills?

Was it lucky to lose
that job before Covid-19
came crashing down and in?

Soon enough, it would seem,
lucky will be reduced to
merely a one-word,

unanswerable,
question.

May ... ...

This is not a time to stop dancing.

~ PW Covington

BOTHER

~ for Karen Honnold
Friday, May 1

Like a bunch o' Pooh Bears
tapping at that raggedy fur
on our raggedy foreheads,

there is too much time now
for thinking thinkally thoughts.

The kind of thoughts that think
themselves, when we don't stop
and think how thinking them
will only lead to other
thinkally thoughts
more bothersome.

Oh, bother… see…?
I'm thinking 'em now.

Here… a news report,
or there… a grandchild.

Everywhere some worry
to worry ourselves ragged.

So many… we no longer
recall what we were first
worrying ourselves about.

To the point that we return
to tapping the raggedy fur
on our raggedy foreheads

as we try to remember…
think… think… think…

"What was it? That first
little thinkally thought
that I was thinking
so much about?"

Thousand-Yard Stare

~ for Jim Donaldson
Saturday, May 2

It's when you can't see
the enemy... and yet—
so clearly—the ghastly
death and godforsaken
destruction in its wake.

The way that destruction
cuts so deep... and yet—
less clearly—so very wide
throughout the world, seen
in the ever-growing, under-
reported number of broken
hearts that fan out in violet
and scarlet waves of debris.

Soldiers, veterans of combat,
have a lot they can teach now,
should they begin to talk again
after everything that happened.

PTSD, soon to be as contagious
as any virus, will need to be caught
early on if our race is to be restored.

The reason some of us have hundreds
of rolls of toilet paper stashed under
every bed, and couch, in the house.

The reason some show up in camo
at government protests, shouldering
fully-loaded semiautomatic weapons.

And the reason nurses block traffic,
standing down the SUVs of restless
citizens.
      And the reason some of us
haven't left our houses—except to
stockpile wine and aged tequila.

We may not be there yet…
but we are starting to see
the signs, there in certain
eyes, and on certain faces.

You Talkin' to Me?

~ for Tim Rutledge
Sunday, May 3

So much more time to talk
now, to that one person,
here in our one place.

Which, strangely,
amounts to less
opportunities
to be heard.

Ever-presence,
like the drone strings
of a sitar... has this way
of making us forget about it.

And only the well-practiced,
like, say, my mom and dad,
married 65 years, in June,
can navigate this Ganges
without map and compass.

Someone we believe we know,
suddenly looks like that tourist
who once stuck his head inside
my car window, in Oklahoma,

and pleaded, "Do! Hep me
fin m'weh to minh str't!"

I thought that, maybe,
I had understood, so...
I pointed to Main Street.

Listening now requires
a strict concentration
we're not sure we are
capable of maintaining.

So we go for long drives
without any sort of where
in mind, or break out a bike,
we say, for exercise. We dream
of a jet that will fly us to, say,
a bullet train that will take us
to, say, a moped in Bordeaux,

so we can want to get to know
again this alien who stands here
before us, as if for the first time.

UNSPOKEN

> ~ for Tina Crittendon Baker
> Monday, May 4

Little hands
don't understand
not being held. Unless,
maybe, they've never felt it.

But let's not speak of that
crime today. Little bodies
were designed for hugs…
and to give big ones back.

Praise be to those things
there's no need to teach.

Mommy hugs squeeze
in a different way than
the hugs from gramma.

We hold grampa's hand
for other reasons than
we do our daddy's,

because it serves as
a separate language,
one older than words.

So here in these days
of our withholding...

with all of the washing,
and all this sanitizing...

followed by so much less
hugging and squeezing...

let's make sure little hearts
are held in the knowing
of a firm love beating
and glowing, here in
our grownup hearts,

until the time comes
when we can, again,
speak in the language
of snuggles and kisses.

AK-47s into Plowshares

~ for Beth Honeycutt
Tuesday, May 5

A moon-sized,
curved, and rusty scythe
of anger and bookless ignorance
is thrashing its mindless resolve
through the acts of kindness
and common sense we pit
against this current dark.

What else for a conscious
soul to do but plant seeds?

The Lotus Flower of Hope
sheds its spore in perpetuity,
and it has a mightier patience,

but the garden must be tended,
a steady watch must be kept.

AK-47s and swastikas
are just broken signals
of entrenched solipsism,
a condition that cannot
even comprehend itself,
because of its blind love.

The connection is lost...
the self-crippling reason
it can't be reasoned with.

That right-angled cross
marches all the way back
to its roots in Sanskrit...
something to do with luck.

But we need more than that.

This will take the cooperation
of our shoulders and elbows,
thighs and knees, all bent
behind the sharpened
plowshare of peace.

And 40 Nights

~ for Gayle Glass
Thursday, May 7

The shyest among the animals
are re-immigrating, two by two,
back to their remembered home-
lands—the national parks that we
deported them from after crushing
beer cans in their faces, then using
their documentation to wipe with.
The skies are clearing—so, they
can navigate by the stars again.
The air is cleaner—so, they can
smell the dearth of our trashed
campsites and smoldering fires.
All the unattended thistles are
blooming and so luscious...
the water, it runs sweet...
the trout have returned
to the pooling eddies.

But .. even the birds,
along with the beasts,
are keeping their eyes
on the ark, because...
they remember well
that long rain.

Where Do We Begin?

> ~ for Donald Trump
> (who did not contribute)
> Friday, May 8

I suppose having a conversation
with you is out of the question.

You've not truly listened to
a thing anyone has said
for decades, if ever.

Though, you have
heard a lot of stuff,
when it's about you.

Stuff you either love,
or hate, depending on
which news anchor it is.

It's just that I'm concerned
about the way your eyes focus
so fiercely on absolutely nothing
that is—as far as we can tell—
actually in the room with us.

I'm wondering if, maybe,
we should try to dig down

and really get to the bottom
of whatever's going on there.

It appears you are more than
just misogynistic—that, maybe,
you're pathologically misanthropic.
I know… you may confuse the two.

Simply put, the second one doubles
your hatred. And look, none of this
is anything we can't be healed of.
I have struggled with the latter
condition for decades now.

But the hardest first step
is—and will always be—

we have to learn how to,
truly, listen to each other.

Quietly, Softly

~ for Ashley
Saturday, May 9

We celebrated
our ninth anniversary
here in our confinement.
A lovely day... a bit warm.

In lieu of store-bought gifts
and flowers, I wrote a poem.

And for the big fancy dinner,
that should be in some pricey
restaurant, I sautéed up a few
scallops in a puddle of butter,
along with exotic mushrooms,
and she roasted a colorful batch
of baby potatoes with rosemary.

And, she appreciated the poem,
in her very quiet sort of manner
that I have come to appreciate,
but not without time and work.

I thought those scallops tasted
better than the twice-as-much
we would have paid for them

in the big and fancy restaurant,
thanks to a few texts, returned
by chef and bud, Konrad Eek.

Our cocktails were also better.

I loved the rosemary potatoes
because I love my Ashley, and
because she's quite a cook too.

There was a softness to it all,
but especially to the scallops
and her exceptional cheeks.

And so it is that we quietly
and softly discovered more
of what we no longer need.

Here's to You

> ~ for Donna Couch, on Mother's Day
> Sunday, May 10

After the many thousands
of days you cared for us,
we devote one to you
in May of each year.

After the countless
times that you bought
and made and brought
us food, we bring to you
this big and beautiful slice
of lemon cake from Legend's.

After those innumerable hugs,
kisses, and the hands you held
over these decades, we will, this
year, celebrate you from a sadly
required distance that pains us,
but the basset hound at home
will make up the difference.

So let us spin a little Garth
and recall all of our friends
that we've had in low places.

And let us raise our glasses –
A margarita, or maybe a Diet
Dr. Pepper, if you'd prefer –
A toast! – To taking care of
you, for a change! – To you!

You, who taught us that size
is no measure of power or
force—nor of endurance.
You, who even the plants
and flowers grow and bloom
under the grace of your touch.
You, who we would never wish
to ever be on the bad side of.
You, who willed so many
of us into almost decency,
if not a half-respectability.
You, who always knew who
to call if we needed windows
cleaned, or our carpets done.
You, who took us in as family,
no matter the circumstances.
You, who taught us of love,
and its much deeper levels.
You, who we owe this,
and every, day… to.

All Lakes Great and Small

~ for Julia Yager
Monday, May 11

Minneapolis has
22 of Minnesota's
10,000 lakes—a number
so rounded, I am suspicious.
But, these 22 seem accounted for.

They even have a Chain of Lakes,
not two miles from downtown,
spreading its links from north
to south, and with names like
Brownie and Bde Maka Ska—
the fattest link and funnest name
to not know how to pronounce.

Having fifteen gorgeous miles
of sidewalks and trails, where
and how do you think folks
are doing their distancing?

A friend tells me there is
no particular time now
to not be out walking.

People seem kinder,
and more encouraging.
The sidewalks themselves
sing with cheery messages like
"Stay positive!" and "Be hopeful!"

Which is not the way southerners
picture northerners, a frostbitten
breed who speak while keeping
their teeth together in order
to conserve a body's heat.

But let's not stereotype.
I know of southerners
who have never once
offered up hospitality.

And yet, it seems to be
on the rise again down here.

We're hosting Happy Hour picnics
out by our fire pit, where the cocktails
keep a careful twelve feet between 'em.

And so what do we say about the parts
of all this that we don't want to lose?

Could we rise, and stay risen,
above the bee-hive, honey-
drunk torpor of brain-
dead consumerism?

Could we begin to see
friendship, walking, and lakes
for the quite enough that they are?

Could it be all the fun we need
to learn the names of those
10,000 lakes, like Pughole,
Weird, Nine AM, Wench,
Jolly Ann, Jock Mock,
Little Too Much, and
Lake Full of Fish?

What the Hand Knows

~ for Sandra Harrington
Wednesday, May 13

The open hand holds more.
It feels more of what it touches
and feels better to another's touch.

How is the heart any different?

The hand burns much less energy
in releasing, and letting go, than
when grabbing and holding on.

How is the mind any different?

The hand that waves hello, wipes
tears, and scratches backs, knows
more than the fist will ever know.

How is the soul any different?

WHAT LUCK

~ for Zee Mink-Fuller
Thursday, May 14

Of course you happen to move
to a new place just days before
the states start turning various
and ominous shades of flames
on national news—indicating
the new numbers of cases...

Of course he has to stay back
at the farm to keep things up
until it sells, so he's not able
to help when the storm hits
and goes all Noah on you,
flooding your new studio
that's a barn, or is it more
like a barn that is a studio?

Of course it's just you, and
the ol' gal-pup, who must
then deal with a rusty hot
water heater gone wonky,
and all the "more water"
that means to a floor...

Of course you swapped
the smooth sandy loam
you worked at the farm
for this glomming black
gumbo gunk—a brand
of soil you didn't know
existed—and so, now,

you're left with globs,
gobs of it, sticking to
shovels, shoes, hands,
and knees, the scraping
and the staining all over
the patio and driveway…

I mean, not everything can
be about pandemics and such.

And Why Not?

> ~ for Catherine Lanham
> Thursday, May 14

So who among us is,
suddenly, up in arms
about having to wear
a mask, who has not
already worn at least
one… if not many…
for most of their secret
and self-denying lives?

Give those of us who
know about ours
a break. Okay?

Most of the time,
most of the masks
we wear affect only
our family and friends.
And more so, our selves.

But now, we are a nuisance,
if not a menace, to the public,
to the children of strangers,
their beloved grandparents.

Wearing that ignorance
on a snot-stained sleeve
is not as invisible as you
want to believe. No mask
will cover up that blotch.

So, in these strange days,
we're offered the chance
to wear a mask of health,
of protection, humanity,
one that says, "I honor
all that's good in you."

And this?   This…
is the one we refuse?

PRAISE BE

~ for Tom Murphy
Friday, May 15

Some do (insert
appropriate adverb)
believe that the economy
rates more important than life.

Nothing new. For centuries now,
those same (insert adjective
of your choice) grubbers
have held commerce
over the dead bodies
of Tasmanian tigers,
passenger pigeons,
or other so-called
inferior species.

But all of a sudden,
those (choose a noun
that best fits your feeling)
have determined that students
and their teachers should be
the next sacrifice we make
to that ambiguous god
of infectious diseases,
wearing its latest crown.

Now that we know voices
kill, let's enclose them then,
in a stuffy fluorescent space
for further heated discussions,
Hallelujah, holy shit! to quote
one of the notable educators
of our time, Clark Griswold.

And so, my friend, who finds
yourself among the condemned,
allow me to join you in telling them
to go (you choose a verb) themselves.

Tom's Parenthetical Suggestions:

> *The High Road*
> Adverb: faithfully
> Adjective: entitled
> Noun: moguls
> Verb: kill

> > *The Low Road*
> > Adverb: absurdly
> > Adjective: greedy
> > Noun: cocksuckers
> > Verb: fuck

FORESIGHT

> ~ for Todd Fuller
> Saturday, May 16

If not with some microbe
hijacking a better cell,
that sick little angel,
tired of his charge,
comes with a blade
he flashes, just out
the corner of an eye,
slitting or tearing its dark
center till the light goes weird.

Then, behind the other good lens,
he seeds a dull cloud that swells,
dimming… dimming… gone.

And what you worry about
first, is the way your children
are, slowly, going out of focus.
Your wife's getting harder to see,
except for that sadness, there,
that is growing in her eyes.

No one understands such
dark meanness, only that
we sometimes wind up

getting the short end
of the sad angel stick.

There's no good way
to look at a thing
you cannot see.
And it won't help
that you're no longer
able to make out a sharp
spike in the current death toll,
or glimpse the idiot masses
gathering in restaurants
without their masks.

Though, a woman
wrote, long ago, of
the superiority of her
blind lover's skills—how,
in seeing her through his hands,
she came to know the ways in which
her other lovers had never seen her at all.

I doubt that's any consolation.
But, my friend, we'll need
to start somewhere.

HOPE

> ~ for Cindy Abbott
> Sunday, May 17

When the moment we live in
tries to choke all the hope
out of us—as the blood-
red, crooked line inches
towards "100,000 Dead"—
it helps to aim what little's left
at smaller, more achievable goals.

Like going ahead and making it
the title of this poem, despite
an English major's concern.

Another example might be:
I hope that precious fawn
comes back to roost again
over in the fire pit tonight.

And I hope my daughter
will continue to revel in
her cup of isolation tea
and quarantine journal,
before or after long walks,
beyond the end of this plague.

I hope my parents make it.

But I also secretly hope
that the rose-skinned,
hairy-backed imbecile
who swaggered his gun
into the grocery store,
like a strap-on dildo,
with no mask to cover
his youtalkin't'me sneer,
comes down with Covid.

I don't need him to die.
I just want him to get
weak enough that he
can't pull the trigger.

Look, we have to allow
a few of those hopes too.
Something to smile about.

I might even dare to hope
that capital-crazed Christians
could learn the very simple math:
   To desecrate God's creation
       is to dishonor God.

But that's a stretch.

Best to stick to
the possible.

Desperate times
call for desperate
metaphors, though
better poets disagree.

But, I'm afraid I'll roast
this old chestnut anyway:

    Hope is a fire.

Collect the kindling.
Chop the wood.
Keep it going.

Silent Mode

~ for Anne Roberts
Monday, May 18

The stage was almost
home for her back then,
negotiating the last decades
of the 20th Century with those
who lived, and died, in its wings.

Her closest friends, talented,
intelligent, young, and gay,
back when our country
had one, clear, line
drawn about it.

So, when death
showed up at the door
of the autoimmune systems
of far too many, she was called
to sing a number at their funerals.

The trauma still lives, like a dormant
disease, in the back of her mind.
And heart. Also, the soul…
things like that do have
a way of spreading.

And that's why, now,
with a modern plague
being the only show
that's still playing
on Broadway,

she feels
a sharp twinge
every single time
her cellphone rings.

All the Wheres Out There

~ for Kiran Cartolari, for his 23rd Birthday
Tuesday, May 19

We are seldom where
we thought we would be.
Oh, I wish I could tell you
that this feeling fades away.
At 55, I like where I am, but
it's not where I thought I'd be.

Life is full of meanwhiles, times
when we must find other ways
to do the same things we love.
We are waiting, now, for some
other place... some other time,
not that where and when we are
is necessarily a bad place or time.

Virgil, and all those great Roman
or Greek storytellers of the ages,
condemned every dutiful hero
to the "three tests," before
they could bear their title.

And so we set out from, say,
Italy, cross some angry ocean,
journey through "life's ways,"

one being to sing the Shades of Brown
up on College Hill in a town called—
can you believe it—Providence?

Then, all of a strange sudden,
we find ourselves in a small
apartment in Manhattan,
taking care of someone
who is worth caring for,
as we fight an invisible foe
that crossed the same ocean
and crawled up the East River.

Turns out, Dante wasn't wrong
when he warned us about losing
the path that does not stray, within
a *savage forest, dense and difficult.*

The thing about hells, though,
at least for the hero, is how they
are meant for us to emerge from.

We will, someday soon enough,
board that fabled ship, sail back
out into the world. But, reborn
with a new sense of who we are,
and all the wheres we want to go.

The Days Are Too Much With Us

~ for William Wordsworth
Thursday, May 21

The days are too much with us; late and soon,
Hemming and hawing, we lay waste our time:
Me, in your hair … and you, all up in mine;
Morning, night, and even, somehow, noon!
We yip, like coyotes, to the sordid moon;
counting the minutes that lead into hours,
Tossing and turning till the midnight sours;
While nightmares tell us, this goes thru June;
We wake up crying – Great God! I'd rather be
Just about anywhere! – Undead! – Or unborn;
Like standing somewhere on some pleasant lea,
Grabbing glimpses of nature's hot pagan porn;
To spot Bo Derek rising naked from the sea;
Or hear old Miles Davis blow his blue horn.

Better than No Place

> ~ for Judith Rycroft
> Friday, May 22

If you ain't where you're at,
you're no place.

> ~ Colonel Potter, M*A*S*H

We did not plan to be
where we happen to be,
right now, when our lives
turned deep shades of blue.

We didn't wake up on some
morning, in 1999, thinking…
You know…? Let's make sure
we do not move to the Lower
East Side in New York, or to,
say, New England, or Jersey.
Because, in about 20 years,
the worst of it will be there.

Just the same, New Yorkers
never thought to think similar
things before the tornados tore
mile-wide holes in the heartland.

We are where we are. And,
Colonel Potter's still right.

Yet, nothing can dampen
the skills of well-practiced
empaths with vivid dreams.

We feel that fevered brow,
we smell that antiseptic…

hear the moans of a child
who does not have its milk.

We see the red eyes of those
whose beloved ones just died
on the other side of the glass.

We taste bedsheets and bile,
and the bad hospital Jell-O
off of some plastic spoon.

So, we do what we can do.
And, we do it where we are,
since we're now not allowed
to be anywhere else anyway.

We wear a mask as a gesture,
because the medical workers,
who are dying too, begged us.

We go without a mocha latte
for a day, a month—besides,
Starbucks, like cockroaches,
will most certainly survive.

And we sit to write a poem
we are not sure will matter,
and yet… we know it does.

We send a prayer, or check.
We wash our hands often.

And we hope that when
the tables are turned…
as tables always do…

those New Yorkers
will return the favor.

A Hint of Vermouth

~ for Konrad Eek
Saturday, May 23

His first odd job at thirteen
as a dishwasher, and busser,
led to a series of odder ones,
until he achieved the oddest:

artist, a master of the lens,
as well as the precise ways
to frame the fallout from it,
so eyes are properly drawn in.

And artists have never needed
a new, improved way to starve.
We are quite gifted in that other
art without the aid of pandemics.

So it is that, when gigs begin to
blink out, like the old taillights
on our Jeep Wrangler ragtop
we drove for 325,000 miles,

we shrug our tired shoulders
and head to the store for extra
bags of beans and brown rice.
Vermouth, gin, rum—staples.

We start to conserve wood,
and toilet paper, and save up
newspapers and old magazines.
You know, for and as backups.

Because, we know what shit
will come—we know how
to dial down to near zero.
And that's why, as others

are still scrambling around,
you'll find us already sitting
in the backyard, twelve feet
apart, sipping gin martinis.

Where the Magic Is

~ for Darra Maxwell-Eek
Sunday, May 24

There's always a magic closet.
Often under stairs. We keep
the princess dolls and quilts
or blankets for building forts
out of couches and cushions
in there, where they're now
stashed away indefinitely…

The number of adventures
that can be sprung deep in,
and out of, a magic closet,
especially between a Mimi
and a whiz of a grandkid,
serve as sound evidence
that money's never been
able to buy what matters.

With a whiff o' Papa Kon's
sausage and scrambled eggs
and powdered-sugar donuts,
still hanging in the warm air,
it's off to another daring do,
some madcap escapade up in
some other part of the house,

somewhere atop those stairs
above that magic closet—
riding on a magic carpet
and singing right along
with that crazy Genie

"I am in the mood
to help you dude.

You ain't never
had a friend
like me."

Hope Springs

~ for Audrey Streetman
Sunday, May 24

The Lenten rose blooms
at winter's end, telling us
things are never too late,
nor ever too early, to rise
from what's cold and dark
into some amount of light.

And it looks as if we'll have
40 days, at least, to ponder
what that might mean to us,
time to consider what going
without meat would've meant
to those with little to begin with.

Now, stores are Open 24 Hours
a Day. Or, even better, Amazon
will put it on a porch tomorrow.

Most Americans honor no season
of self-sacrifice these days… no
prescribed wildernesses either.

We fail to contemplate that,
if God's son considered it

a necessity, then maybe we
underestimate its worth, no?

No, here in the Land of Oz
every day is a Fat Tuesday.

Could it be, come some
holy day, that which saves
us from our comfort, might
be the very thing that saves us,
finally, from selfish blindness?

We trudge through these days
with Lenten faces, mourning
the loss of some thing long
forgotten. And yet we know
that whatever it was, we once
felt so sad that it had to leave.

So we stand here half-believing,
if we stay and stare long enough,
we may remember what that was,
and it will rise like this Lenten rose.

The Newness

~ for Pam Melson
Monday, May 25

So where does a nurse go
to heal from one of life's
greater divides? 40 years
you give to a town, and
a man. And, suddenly,

you're thumbing back
through the textbooks
of mental health courses
that *you* have been teaching,
wondering if it's time, maybe,
to take some of their advice?

Life checks us now and then
to see if our systems are on
and operating consciously.

Sort of the way, in Texas,
we stick habanero pepper
in New York Cheesecake,
to keep dessert honest—
a little less full of itself.

So you moved, in order
to be close to a daughter
and that sweet, new baby.
Classes have been canceled.
The daughter's back to work.

And now it's you and this new
life—the tiny one in your arms
and the big one beating again
in your chest—taking care
of each other—a new life
has never felt so possible.

A blossoming strength
is pleasantly strange…
an unexpected coup.

And, lo and behold,
you discovered that
doing unto yourself
what you have been
doing for others is…

just one more way to
spread the goodness.

What Makes Sons

~ for Myra Spector
Wednesday, May 27

There's always the one who
can explain what is wrong
with the stock exchange
and why you shouldn't
worry about it anyway.

The one just in from, say,
Europe, or was it Australia
this time? God, who knows?

This one's calm, talks recipes,
needed close to no help at all
in growing up, raised himself
in an almost spooky silence.

Then, there is the one who
can tell you what is broken
up on Capitol Hill (so much
is) and yet, why it's a waste
of good time to believe we,
or anyone, could ever fix it.

This one loves… laughs…
keeps you rolling in both,

while scaring you to death
with what he might do next.

Not the least of which could
be fighting against injustice...
standing for dignity and rights.

This is why The Fates so often
dole out sons in twos—maybe
threes. Mothers would be far
too much for one to handle.

The mothers who become
the reason that some sons
go out into the wild world
and try to save it—despite
the evidence, and the odds.

LIKE IT IS

> ~ for Ivan Kohlman, for his 24th Birthday
> Thursday, May 28

*Who are these people,
and why am I here?*

I said that to myself
with varying degrees
of consciousness all
through the middle
and high school days.

The artist often lives
the lonely life before
becoming that artist.

And I'll call the artist
storyteller from here on.
It's more what I mean.

So, the storyteller can't
stand to ever be "told"
what to think or how to
do this, that or the other.

It is our story, our poem,
our film, and we will tell it,

by God, the way we want,
and no amount of filling in
little circles with A, B, C, D,
and E in all caps inside them
is going to teach us a better
way to tell our unique story.

Only good teachers, sages,
can do that. I recall one,
in particular, in 7th grade.

A few professors at OU
changed me… forever.

And I rate travel among
the greatest I've ever had.

Nothing, though, compares
to the efficacy of hard failure.

The world claims to treasure
its artists—and yet, it shuns
the souls that are struggling
to become one. They want
us to pop out of the shell,
somehow, as a hot combo
of Spielberg and Tarantino.

> (And, what a marriage
> in hell that would be.)

Of course the frustration
over this absurdity is key
to our ultimate education.

If I've lost you, I'm sorry,
but… struggling artists are
high on my list of priorities.

Maybe I'll write you another
poem, on some other day?

For now I will finish with
an unforgivable platitude:

> Civilization will perish
> without better stories.

The Effect It Has

> Friday, May 29

The Dunning-Kruger effect,
brought to us by concerned
psychologists in need of new
human defects to research—

a project they likely brewed up
over beers and cigars in a bar—

explains the phenomenon of how
certain individuals with an inferior
ability at a given task, frequently
hold to a delusional belief that
their ability is, in fact, superior.

The psychologists said it comes
from thinking "without the self-
awareness of metacognition."

But, I have an inferior ability
to comprehend academia's love
for obfuscation and pleniloquence.

So let's put this in the plain speak
of my psychologist, who tells me
it means, in essence, that certain

stupid people are just too stupid
to appreciate how stupid they are.

A bit harsh, and yet no less pointed
than Dunning and Kruger saying
that this "bias results from an
internal illusion," or worse,

"the miscalibration of the
incompetent stems from
an error about the self."

My therapist and I
had been discussing
a voting demographic
at the time.

            However,
I now can't stop thinking
of all the posers who write
poems without bothering
to read much better ones.

Dancing with Saint Vitus

~ for Becky Eagleton Hinshaw
Saturday, May 30

There are more animal
moments of vital breath
when our movement slips
from the voluntary into
the involuntary—

a space just beyond
the physics of reason
where our entire body
can be swung around by
a single strand of our hair.

It's cabin fever run amuck
in the hills of imagination.

The leg-spread of abandon,
risking that foot to the crotch
from the dancer right behind us.

We are, unofficially, no longer here,
but over in some unknown there.

Limbs and torsos unbound by
ligament, muscle, and bone.

The spirit has left the basilica,
and run out into the empty streets
to proclaim that we were not meant
to live by bread or cooped up all alone.

It's religion's quarantine of the soul
resisting its foregone conclusion.

It's when the cats start shaking
their furry booties with us,
without knowing why.

And this wild dance
has been known to
last for only seconds,

or in my bizarre case
of stacking stones,

years.

OH, JONATHAN

~ for Jonathan Karl
White House Correspondent
Sunday, May 31

You stumbled over
your follow-up question...

since the shock was still frozen
to your face from his answer
to the initial question.

Understandable.

You've got a job to do,
and we see you struggling.

It can be painful to watch...
well... him... more than you.

And look... a pat on the back
from a poet won't buy a latte.

But it seems someone needs
to cheer you on... and up.

The Ritual

> ~ for Carol Naifeh
> In Honor of Robert N. Naifeh, Jr.
> Monday, June 1

Our lives, as they tend to,
move on, and time, as poets
have said since its beginning,
flows on, like a turgid river.

But the 29th day of March
in 2020, doesn't budge.
It stays, stubbornly,
right where it was.

Right where we barely
got to say our goodbyes—
in the required armor of the ICU
that is tough to remember, or forget.

And now the separations, from the one
who left but also the ones left behind,
become like all unbearable griefs…
that must be borne nonetheless.

There are the conversations,
with him, as well as the others.

But with him now, there's more
of just listening... on both sides.

At the same time, it often seems
that the quieter the messages are,
the more we listen to their intent,
the more power they have to help.

And so it is that time, in its ever-
swelling surge toward wherever
it's so compelled to keep going,
encourages us to begin thinking

about what he would have wanted.
And we will repeat it to each other
in a soft, but a hard-felt, ritual...
until it becomes what we want.

Also by Nathan Brown

*Just Another Honeymoon in France:
    A Vagabond at Large*
100 Years
An Honest Day's Prayer
An Honest Day's Ode
An Honest Day's Confession
*I Shouldn't Say…The Mostly Unedited
    Poems of Ezra E. Lipschitz*
*Arse Poetica: The Mostly Unedited
    Poems of Ezra E. Lipschitz*
*Apocalypse Soon: The Mostly Unedited
    Poems of Ezra E. Lipschitz*
Don't Try (with Jon Dee Graham)
*My Salvaged Heart:
    Story of a Cautious Courtship*
*To Sing Hallucinated:
    First Thoughts on Last Words*
Oklahoma Poems, and Their Poets
Less Is More, More or Less
Karma Crisis: New and Selected Poems
Letters to the One-Armed Poet
My Sideways Heart
Two Tables Over
Not Exactly Job
Ashes over the Southwest
Suffer the Little Voices
Hobson's Choice

Author Bio

Nathan Brown is an author, songwriter, and award-winning poet living in Wimberley, Texas. He holds a PhD in English and Journalism from the University of Oklahoma and taught there for over twenty years. He also served as Poet Laureate for the State of Oklahoma in 2013 and 2014.

He's published over 20 books. Among them is *100 Years, To Sing Hallucinated: First Thoughts on Last Words,* and *Don't Try,* a collection of poems co-written with songwriter and Austin Music Hall-of-Famer, Jon Dee Graham. His anthology *Oklahoma Poems, and Their Poets* was a finalist for the Oklahoma Book Award. *Karma Crisis: New and Selected Poems* was a finalist for the Paterson Poetry Prize. And his earlier book, *Two Tables Over,* won the 2009 Oklahoma Book Award. He has also released several CDs of original music.

For more, go to: **brownlines.com**

MEZCALITA PRESS

An independent publishing company
dedicated to bringing the printed poetry,
fiction, and non-fiction of musicians who
want to add to the power and reach
of their important voices.

www.ingramcontent.com/pod-product-compliance
Lightning Source LLC
Chambersburg PA
CBHW020928090426
42736CB00010B/1073